D0833601

95 0249076 7

THE 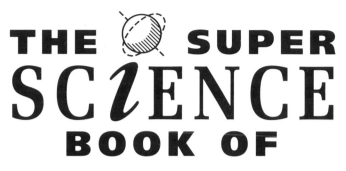 SUPER SCIENCE BOOK OF SPACE

Jerry Wellington

How Big is Space?

If you're small like me,
You don't take up much space.
But Jupiter, Mars

And all of the stars

Need a lot more space
than the
human race.

I suppose that's why they're in a place

Just full of S P A C E.

Illustrations by Frances Lloyd

Wayland

Titles in the Super Science series

The Environment
Light
Materials
Our Bodies
Sound
Space
Time
Weather

The Super Science Book of Space

This book is full of interesting ideas and facts about space, and it explores all sorts of subjects – the universe, looking at stars and planets, legends of the stars, famous astronomers and astronauts, how spacecraft work, and life on Earth and in space.

Whether you choose to dip into this book, try out some of the simple activities or sit down and read it from cover to cover, the *Super Science Book of Space* will show you that science can be fun.

Series Editor: James Kerr
Editor: Alison Field
Designer: Loraine Hayes Design
Consultant: Jane Battell, Advisory Teacher for Science in East Sussex, Key Stages 1, 2 and 3

First published in 1993 by Wayland (Publishers) Ltd
61 Western Road, Hove, East Sussex, BN3 1JD, England

British Library Cataloguing in Publication Data
Wellington, J. J.
    Super Science Book of Space.—(Super Science Series)
    I. Title II. Martin, Gordon III. Series
    523.1

ISBN 0 7502 0636 5

Typeset by Dorchester Typesetting Group Ltd
Printed and bound by L.E.G.O. in Italy

Acknowledgements

Dennis Ashton for his contribution on Star Gazing.
Hannah and Becky Wellington for help with all parts of the book.
Sue Clewes for help in preparing the text.

Illustrations by Frances Lloyd.
Cover illustration by Martin Gordon.

Photographs by permission of: Ann Ronan Picture Library 9 top, 16 bottom, 21; Dennis Ashton 19 top; Eye Ubiquitous 9 bottom, 15 bottom, 26, 29; Science Photo Library 10, 11, 15 top, 16 top, 17, 19 bottom, 20, 22, 23, 27; ZEFA 24, 28.

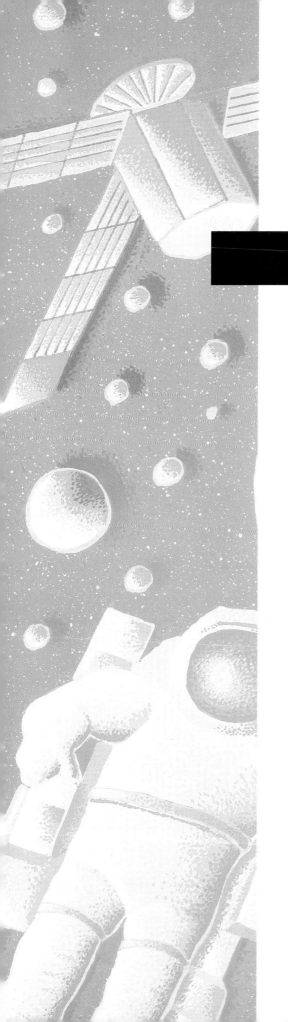

CONTENTS

WHAT IS SPACE?

Imagine you go for a journey in a ▶ balloon. You gradually rise higher into the sky, up as high as the clouds. How do you feel? Well, first of all you get colder! Every time you rise by 150 m, the temperature drops by about 1 degree Celsius (1°C). The other thing that happens is that the higher you go, the thinner the air gets and the less oxygen there is to breathe. There is less air above you, and the air pressure is much lower than at sea-level.

On Earth we live underneath a huge blanket of air that stretches for many kilometres upwards. This means that the air on Earth has pressure. It pushes on everything around us.

Find Out about Air Pressure

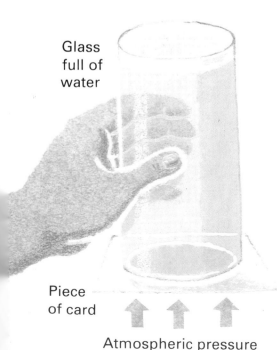

Glass full of water

Piece of card

Atmospheric pressure

1 Fill a glass or jam-jar right to the brim with water.

2 Place a card over the top, make sure there are no air bubbles inside, then turn the jar upside down.

3 What happens? The air pressure keeps the card in place and is strong enough to support the water – as long as there are no air bubbles inside the jar to press the other way.

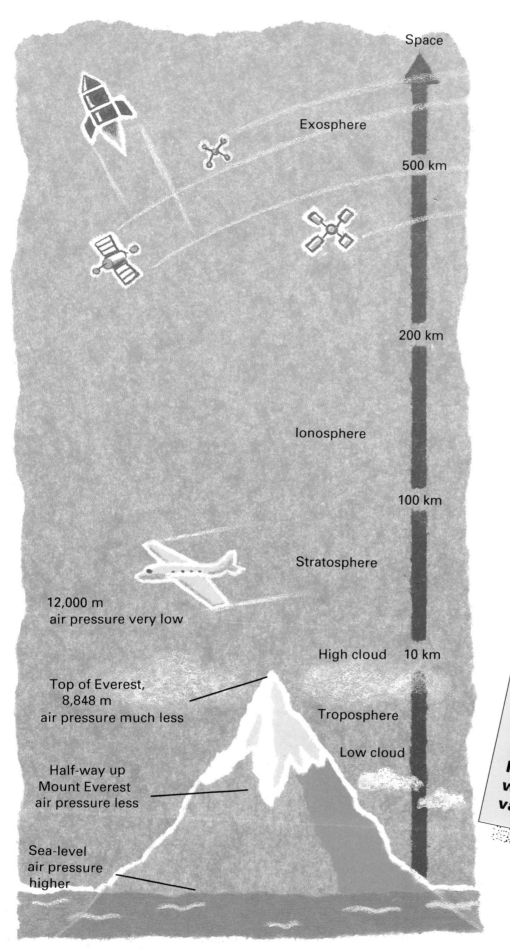

Space

Exosphere

500 km

200 km

Ionosphere

100 km

Stratosphere

12,000 m
air pressure very low

High cloud   10 km

Top of Everest,
8,848 m
air pressure much less

Troposphere

Low cloud

Half-way up
Mount Everest
air pressure less

Sea-level
air pressure
higher

◄   The blanket of air that surrounds the Earth and keeps you alive is called the atmosphere. As you rise higher above the Earth, you go above the clouds into different layers of the atmosphere. Just above the cloud is a layer called the stratosphere, then the ionosphere and then the exosphere. Eventually you reach space. If you could travel far enough into space, there would be no air at all, and you would escape from the pull of the Earth's gravity.

WOW!
It might be hard to make a good cup of tea at the top of Mount Everest. Water in a kettle boils at only 60°C there, instead of 100°C at sea-level. The air pressure is much lower at that height, so liquid water turns to vapour more easily.

HOW DID THE UNIVERSE BEGIN?

The universe is everything – the Moon, the Sun, our galaxy, other galaxies . . . and all the space in between. Many scientists believe that the universe began with a big bang! The material of the universe exploded outwards to form the dark space, stars, galaxies and planets you can see today.

Scientists estimate that the big bang ▶ happened about 17,000 million years ago – it's hard to imagine, isn't it? About four to five thousand million years ago our solar system and the Earth were formed, and then life began to appear on our planet.

Human beings are a very new feature of the universe. If you imagine the life of the universe as a 24-hour clock, humans have probably been around for less than half an hour.

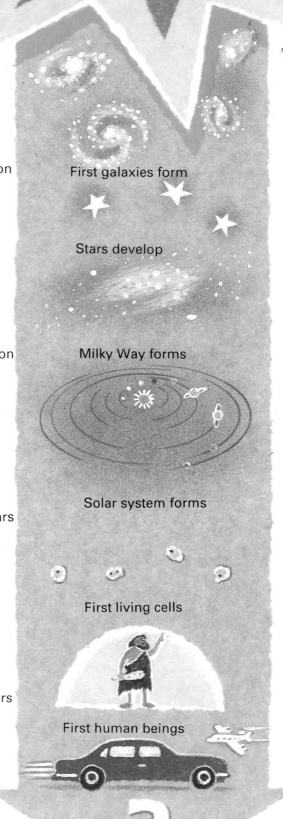

1,000 million years — First galaxies form

Stars develop

5,000 million years — Milky Way forms

10,000 million years — Solar system forms

First living cells

15,000 million years

First human beings

Today

The future

The universe is so enormous that it is almost impossible to imagine its size. Scientists believe that it is still getting bigger from the force of the big bang.

Astronauts often measure distances in space in 'light-years'. One light-year is the distance travelled by light in a single year. Light travels 300,000 km in one second – so how far is one light-year in kilometres? Try it on your calculator: 300,000 km × 365 days × 24 hours × 60 minutes × 60 seconds.

Imagine you leave Earth and travel ▶ at the speed of light to the edge of the universe. You pass the Moon in one and a half seconds, and the Sun after eight and a half minutes. You leave the solar system after five hours. After four and a half years you pass the nearest star after the Sun, and eventually leave our galaxy after 2,000 years.

WOW!
The nearest star to Earth is Proxima Centauri, 4.3 light-years away. The light we see from this star left it 4.3 years ago.

A neighbour of our galaxy is the Andromeda galaxy, about two million light-years away. This is just one of the billions of galaxies in the universe. To reach the edge of the universe will take you another 15,000 million years.

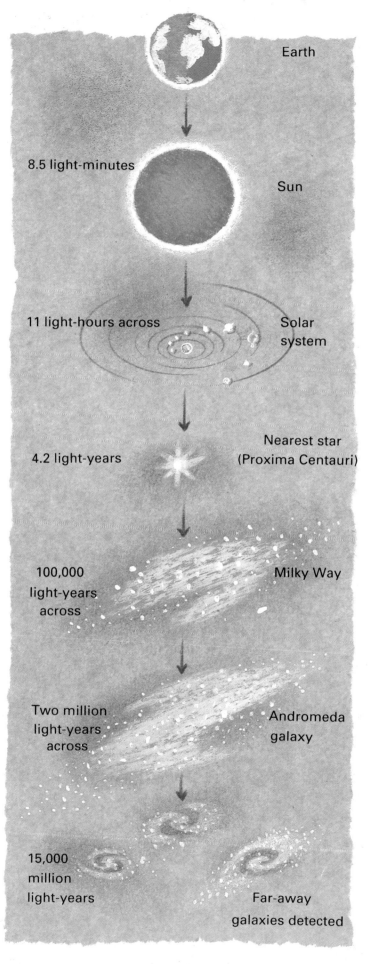

Earth

8.5 light-minutes — Sun

11 light-hours across — Solar system

4.2 light-years — Nearest star (Proxima Centauri)

100,000 light-years across — Milky Way

Two million light-years across — Andromeda galaxy

15,000 million light-years — Far-away galaxies detected

WATCHING THE MOON

If you look up into space on a clear ▶ night, you will see the Moon, nearly 400,000 km from Earth. The Moon has no light of its own – we see it because sunlight falls on it and the Moon reflects it back. As the Moon goes round the Earth, we see different phases of the Moon, depending on how much light is reflected back to our position on Earth. We might see a full moon, a half moon, a crescent moon or a new moon.

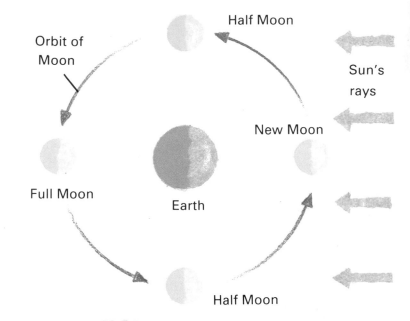

If you look closely at the ▶ Moon through a telescope or binoculars, you will see that it is covered in deep craters. Newton, the deepest, is nearly 9 km deep. In between the craters are large 'seas'. Ancient astronomers thought they were oceans – but now we know there is no air, no water, no wind and no weather of any kind on the Moon. It is a lifeless place.

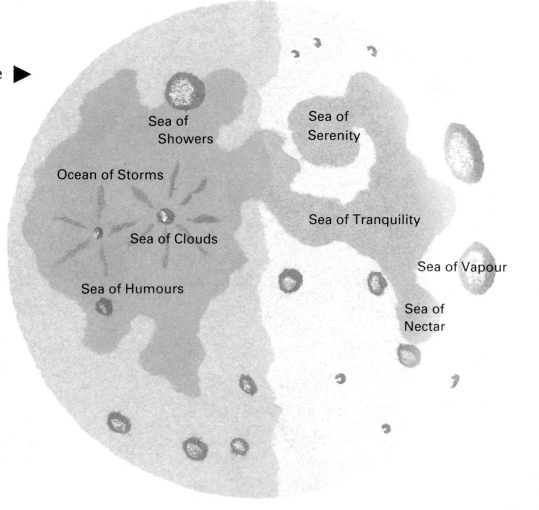

◀ The Moon takes just under twenty-eight days to go once round the Earth. We call this a 'lunar month'. In exactly the same time, the Moon spins once round on its axis. This means that from Earth we always see the same side of the Moon. Its dark side is always hidden to us. Thanks to space travel we now know that the dark side of the Moon has even deeper craters and higher mountains than the side we see. It has no large seas.

In 1969, two American astronauts ▶ became the first people to walk on the Moon's surface. How do you think it felt? Well, the Moon's gravity is six times weaker than the Earth's. If the astronauts had been high jumpers on Earth, they could have jumped more than 10 m on the Moon – if they hadn't been wearing spacesuits!

WOW!
Can you see the footprints left by the first astronauts on the Moon? They will still be there one hundred years – even one million years – from now. There is no wind, rain or person to spoil them.

OUR NEAREST STAR

Stars are giant balls of gas. The Sun, 150 million km
from Earth, is our star – without it there would be no
life on Earth.

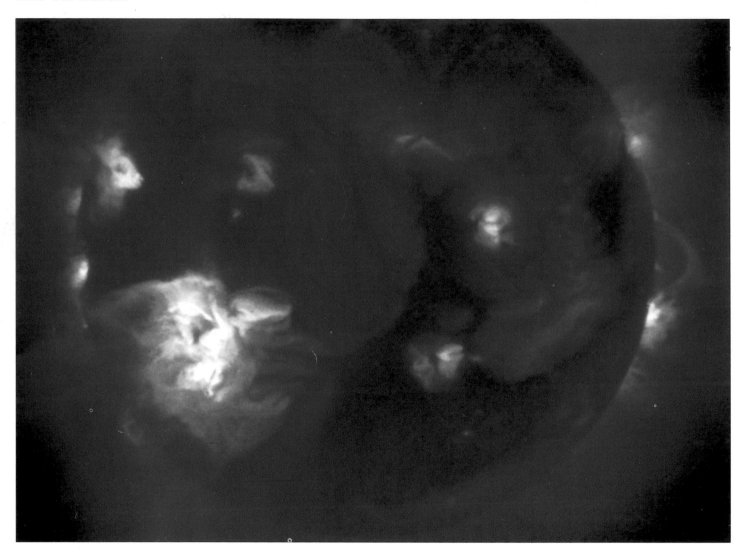

▲ The Sun is an amazing object. It is
larger than a million Earths. Inside the
Sun the temperature is 15 million °C,
at the surface it is about 6,000°C. It
uses up about 700 million tonnes of
hydrogen every second. But don't
worry – it should last for another 5,000
million years. Then it will start to
become larger and redder. It will turn
into a 'Red Giant', and then gradually
shrink to become a 'White Dwarf'.

You should never look directly at the
Sun – its radiation can seriously
damage your eyes. If you look at the
Sun through a piece of darkened glass,
or a dark plastic filter, you will see
dark spots on its surface. These are
called sunspots and are slightly colder
than the rest of the Sun's surface. The
Sun spins around once every twenty-
seven days, so the position of these
spots changes.

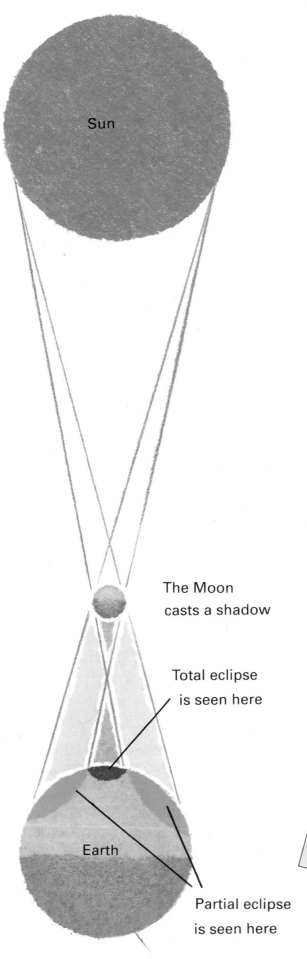

Sun

The Moon
casts a shadow

Total eclipse
is seen here

Earth

Partial eclipse
is seen here

◄ Sometimes the Moon passes between the Sun and the Earth, and blocks out some of the Sun's rays. The Moon then casts a shadow on the Earth's surface. If someone on the Earth is in the middle of this shadow, they see a total eclipse. Towards the edges of the shadow, a person looking up sees a black area passing across the surface of the Sun – this is called a partial eclipse.

▲ If you're ever lucky enough to see a total eclipse, you will be able to look up at the Sun and see its corona. The centre of the Sun looks black but, around the edge, extending out into space, is the Sun's corona. This is a beautiful, bright, glowing area all around our own star, the Sun.

WOW!
If you used a marble to represent the size of the Earth, you would need a large beach ball to show the size of the Sun.

WATCHING THE SUN

The Sun seems to come up, or rise, in the East, and go down, or set, in the West. This happens because the Earth spins round. As it spins, your part of the Earth faces the Sun for some of the time – this is daytime. At night-time, the place where you are faces away from the Sun.

North
Earth spins round this axis
Daytime here
sunlight
Equator
sunlight
Night-time here
South

The Earth travels in a curved path, its orbit, around the Sun. The imaginary line through the middle of the Earth, its axis, is slightly tilted. When the northern part of the Earth is tilted away from the Sun, that part (the northern hemisphere) has its winter, and the southern hemisphere has its summer.

Earth spins
Northern autumn
Southern spring
Northern winter
Equator
Northern summer
Equator
Sun
Southern winter
Southern summer
Northern spring
Southern autumn

The Earth takes 365 and a quarter days to go once round the Sun. Our calendar lasts for 365 days, and we add the extra quarters together until we have enough for one extra day, making a leap year every four years of 366 days.

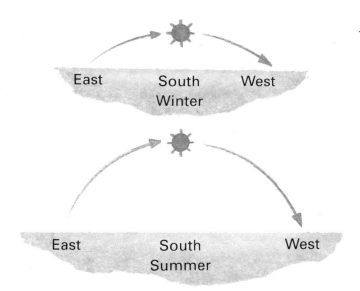

East   South   West
Winter

East   South   West
Summer

◀ As the Earth goes round in its orbit, the height of the Sun changes. In the midwinter sky, when the Earth is tilted away, the Sun is low in the sky. It rises later and sets earlier. In midsummer the opposite happens. The Sun looks much higher in the sky, and the days last longer. Half-way between midsummer and midwinter, we have equal days and equal nights (equinox).

Study the Sun's Elevation

1 Push a straight stick through a large piece of white cardboard and into the ground.
2 Face the card away from the Sun.
3 With a pencil or pen, mark the position and length of the Sun's shadow at different times of day. What do you think you will see? When will the shadow be shortest?

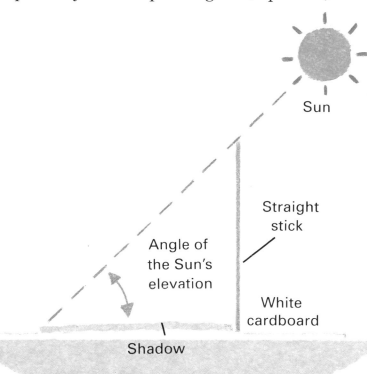

Sun

Straight stick

Angle of the Sun's elevation

White cardboard

Shadow

White cardboard

Straight stick

Sun

Shadow

The shadow changes throughout the day – from long to short and back to long again. The shorter the shadow, the higher the Sun's height, or elevation. Try this experiment in summer and in winter. How do you think the midday shadow in winter will compare with the midday shadow in summer?

THE SUN'S FAMILY

The Sun has a family of nine planets that orbit around it. The Sun and its planets are called the solar system.

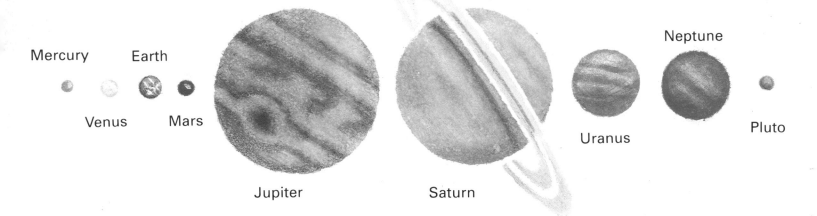

Mercury Earth

Venus Mars

Jupiter

Saturn

Uranus

Neptune

Pluto

Look at these facts about the Sun's family of planets.

What is its name?	Roughly how big is it compared with Earth?	How far is it from the Sun? (in millions of km)	How hot is it on the surface? (in °C)	How long does it take to go round the Sun?	How many moons does it have?
Mercury	one-third	58	350	88 days	0
Venus	two-thirds	108	480	225 days	0
Earth	—	150	22	365 days	1
Mars	half	228	−23	2 years	2
Jupiter	eleven times	778	−150	12 years	16
Saturn	nine times	1,425	−180	29 years	17
Uranus	four times	2,867	−210	84 years	15
Neptune	almost four times	4,486	−220	164 years	2
Pluto	one-third	5,900	−230	248 years	1

---

* Which planets are bigger than Earth?
* Which is the biggest planet of all?
* Which planet has the hottest surface?
* Which planet takes the longest to go round the Sun?

* Which planet do we think has the most moons?
* What do you notice about the number of moons compared with the size of the planets?

Two really big and beautiful planets are Jupiter and Saturn. Spacecraft without people in have travelled close to Jupiter and Saturn and have come back with beautiful pictures. The longest spacecraft missions took over ten years because the spacecraft had to travel so far – Saturn is ten times farther from the Sun than the Earth is.

▲ Can you see the great Red Spot on Jupiter? This is a giant whirling storm, three times as big as the Earth.

◀ These planets also have moons or satellites. Look at Saturn's famous rings. They are made of lumps of ice, circling round Saturn like tiny moons.

We now know that planets travel round the Sun in a path rather like a flattened circle. This path is called an ellipse.

Draw an Ellipse

1 Pin a sheet of paper ▶ onto a soft board and tie some strong thread round two drawing pins to make a loop.
2 Put a pencil inside the loop and draw right round, keeping the thread tight. You have drawn an ellipse, the same shape as a planet's orbit.

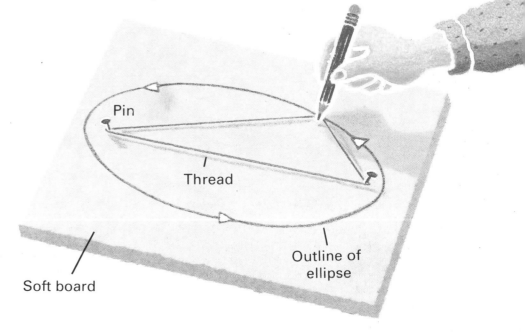

Pin

Thread

Outline of ellipse

Soft board

COMETS AND GALAXIES

We have looked at the Sun's family – now it is time to take a journey through the solar system and out into the far reaches of the universe. The first thing you would notice if you travelled through the solar system is that it is a very messy place. It is not as neat and tidy as it looks in pictures. The solar system is full of lumps and bits flying around.

Pieces of rock called asteroids, some as large as small planets, orbit round the Sun. These are the leftovers from the time the solar system was formed. Some lumps of rock and ice move round the Sun in very strangely shaped orbits. These large, dirty snowballs are called comets.

▲ The most famous is Halley's Comet, which can be seen from the Earth every seventy-six years. The photograph shows how it looked in 1910 from Peru.

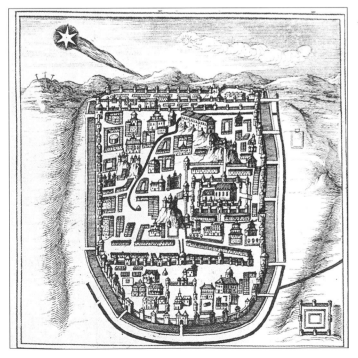

◄ Halley's Comet was first spotted centuries ago. This old drawing shows how it looked to people from Jerusalem in AD 66. If you're still alive in 2062, you will be able to see it.

WOW!
Some people believe that UFOs (unidentified flying objects) seen from Earth are signs that there is life elsewhere in the universe. Every day more than forty sightings of UFOs are reported.

▲ Our Sun is just one of thousands of millions of stars in a collection called a galaxy. Our galaxy is called the Milky Way and forms a beautiful spiral shape.

◄ The next galaxy is called the Andromeda galaxy, which is more than two million light-years away, but it can be seen without a telescope. It is another spiral galaxy.

The universe has millions of other galaxies. People often wonder whether there are other solar systems with life in them, just like our own. Many scientists believe that the chance of life existing elsewhere in the universe is very high. What do you think? Could life outside Earth be similar to life here?

STAR GAZING

Star patterns are called constellations. They are like dot-to-dot pictures in the sky.

The Plough is the most famous star ▶ pattern of all. It looks like a giant saucepan. Can you see the handle and the pan? The two stars called the pointers show the way to the Pole Star. The Plough is really part of a bigger constellation called the Great Bear.

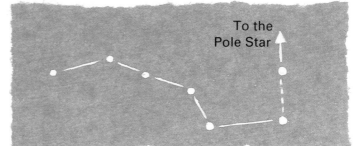

Looking North

Our sky map shows some of the winter constellations. ▼

Orion is the hunter. The three stars in a line make his belt. Betelgeuse and Rigel are his brightest stars.

Procyon and Sirius are stars in Orion's hunting dogs. Sirius is the brightest star in the night sky.

Taurus is the head of the bull, with Aldebaran as his angry red eye. Taurus is the home of the Seven Sisters star cluster.

Auriga the Charioteer and the two Gemini twins, Castor and Pollux, complete the set of Orion's friends.

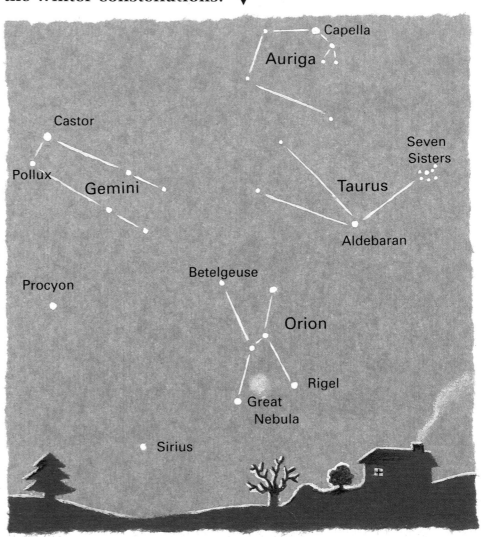

Looking South

Look at the Stars

You can see lots of things without a telescope – though binoculars will help.
Try these:
* the colours of Betelgeuse, Rigel, Aldebaran and Capella
* the Seven Sisters star cluster
* the great Orion nebula
* shooting stars (meteors).

▲ Orion and his companions are in the sky during winter. Can you see the shooting star?

Astronomers use telescopes to look at stars, nebulae and galaxies. Telescopes collect more light than our eyes do. They make dim objects look much brighter and clearer. ▼

Infra-red telescopes in satellites can look inside nebulae for the heat from stars actually being born. Other satellites carry x-ray telescopes to search for black holes.

Other kinds of telescopes can detect radiation that we cannot see. Radio telescopes pick up radio signals from space. Radio telescopes have discovered pulsars, the remains of exploded stars. They have also found quasars, the most distant objects in our universe.

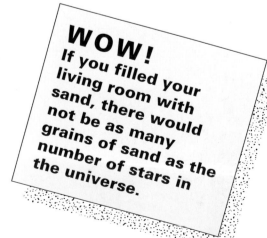

WOW!
If you filled your living room with sand, there would not be as many grains of sand as the number of stars in the universe.

GREAT STAR GAZERS

People have been gazing into the sky for as long as there have been people. The ancient Chinese observed eclipses of the Sun and Moon around three or four thousand years BC.

In the second century ► AD, an Egyptian called Ptolemy said that the Earth is at the centre of the universe, with the Sun going round it.

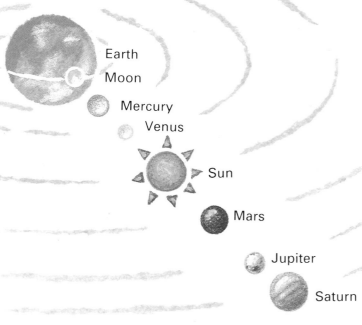

Earth
Moon
Mercury
Venus
Sun
Mars
Jupiter
Saturn

◄ Most people believed this view of the universe for about the next 1,300 years. Then, in 1543, a Polish astronomer called Nicolas Copernicus said that Ptolemy was wrong and that the Sun is actually at the centre of our solar system. Most people couldn't believe it.

About fifty years later, Copernicus' idea was supported by an Italian scientist called Galileo. In 1609 he built one of the first telescopes and used it to look at the Moon, the planets and the Milky Way. In the drawing, Galileo is showing off his telescope in Venice.

Galileo's observations led him to believe that it was impossible that everything should go round the Earth. Galileo disagreed with the Roman Catholic Church, who believed that Ptolemy had been right. Poor Galileo was kept under guard in his house in Italy until he died in 1642. The Church forgave him in 1980!

Another famous astronomer, who was born in the year that Galileo died, was Sir Isaac Newton. He studied the motion of the planets and suggested many of the laws about movement and gravity that we still use today. He first explained that gravity extends right through space and is the force that keeps the planets in their curved orbits. Newton made a special reflecting telescope that used mirrors.

▼

▲ In the eighteenth century a sister and brother called Caroline and William Herschel made telescopes to observe the planets and stars. They discovered the planet Uranus in 1781. This 13 m telescope was built by them.

BACK DOWN TO
EARTH

The Earth is the most beautiful of all the planets. It is probably the only planet that could support life, because it has two important things: air and water.

From space ▶ we can look back on the Earth and study its surface. You can see that it looks like a blue and white globe – what do you think the white parts are? Can you see North and South America through the clouds? More than two thirds of the Earth's surface is covered in sea water.

Around the Earth is the blanket of air that keeps us alive. The atmosphere and clouds protect us in several ways. They stop the temperatures on Earth from becoming too high or too low – imagine how hot it would be in the day without the atmosphere and how cold it would be at night.

One important part of the Earth's atmosphere contains a gas called ozone. This part, called the ozone layer, protects us from some of the Sun's harmful rays. Although it is many kilometres above the Earth, we need to take great care of this protective layer. Chemicals called CFCs have made the layer thinner and even caused a hole in it. Damage to the ozone layer can be very dangerous to people, other animals and some plants.

▲ In space there are thousands of tiny missiles flying around. These are called 'shooting stars' when they fly into the Earth's atmosphere and burn up. But the atmosphere cannot protect us from all bombardment from outer space. A giant meteor once smashed against the Earth in Arizona in the USA and left this giant crater, 1 km wide and 200 m deep. Without the atmosphere, the Earth would be covered in these craters, just like the Moon.

WOW!
Death Valley in California can be as hot as 45°C, while Siberia can get as cold as −50°C. But this is nothing compared to Mars. Daytime temperatures reach 400°C, hot enough to melt lead. At night it drops to −200°C – pretty chilly!

JOURNEY TO A
SPACE STATION

Ten, nine, eight, seven, six . . .

When a spacecraft takes off, its rocket engines gradually build up their pushing force until it is larger than the weight of the entire rocket and spacecraft. When this happens, liftoff begins!

As the force of the engines gets bigger, the rocket picks up speed. About twelve seconds into takeoff, the astronauts begin to feel g forces, a bit like when you are pushed into the back of your seat in a plane as it is taking off. But in the rocket, the forces build up until the astronauts feel three times as heavy as they do on Earth. They can hardly raise an arm.

After all the rockets have been ignited and burnt, there is a sudden drop to weightlessness. When the spacecraft is close enough to the space station, the two are joined together.

To attach the spacecraft to the space station, special rocket engines give short blasts that gradually push the craft into position, like a ship mooring at harbour. In their weightless state, the astronauts pull themselves through an opening into the station.

The *Mir* station orbits the Earth sixteen times a day. In other words, each orbit takes about one and a half hours. The astronauts experience sixteen dark times and sixteen light times in their day – it must be hard to stay asleep! They travel at a speed of 8 km per second – fast enough to go from London to Brighton in ten seconds.

To get back down to Earth, the craft is disconnected from the station. Then, engines are fired and the craft descends towards the Earth. The astronauts feel those forces again – up to five times their own weight. As the craft re-enters the Earth's atmosphere, the friction with the air heats up the outside, like the burning of a climber's hands from sliding down a nylon rope.

◀ High in the air, a parachute opens and the craft slows down. Just before landing, the craft fires special rockets backwards to soften the landing. Splashdown!

WOW!
If astronauts travelled at the speed of light, they could circle the Earth seven times in one second.

LIVING IN A
SPACE STATION

Living in space is different! Astronauts feel as if they have no weight at all. They 'float around' inside their craft – there is no difference between up and down, floor and ceiling.

This often gives the astronauts space sickness, a feeling like sea sickness. Without weight, the blood and other liquids in their bodies go towards their heads – many astronauts have red, puffy cheeks for the first few days in space until their bodies get used to it.

They also get taller by a few centimetres – can you guess why? Here's a hint: in space, there is no weight pressing down on their spines.

Astronauts must breathe, so the space station is filled with the same air that we breathe on Earth. The air is circulated round the craft and kept fresh using special fans and filters.

They also have to eat and drink. Special food is taken up to the station. This is the kind of diet that a modern astronaut might have. Not bad, is it?

Breakfast	Canned meatloaf, bread, chocolate sweets with nut praline, coffee with milk, prune juice
Lunch	Canned beef, tongue, bread, prunes with nuts ·
Dinner	Caspian roach (fish), bortsch (soup), canned veal, bread, rich pastry, blackcurrant juice
Supper	Cream cheese with blackcurrant purée, canned fruit, blackcurrant juice

◀ The astronauts find it easier to eat if they are held down by special stirrups. The food needs to be held down too, using elastic straps.

After all this eating, drinking and floating, you can guess what astronauts need to do! Each day they produce these waste products:

* 2.5 kg of urine
* 0.8 kg of carbon dioxide from breathing out
* 0.2 kg of solid waste (faeces).

◄ The astronauts go to a special toilet that 'sucks' the waste out into space – can you imagine what would happen if they used water to flush it away? (Remember – there is no weight in space.) Sometimes their urine is recycled and turned back into water to be used again, but this happens only on a long flight.

Design an Astronaut Exercising Machine

In space, astronauts need to exercise to stay fit and healthy while they are weightless.

Design an astronaut exercising machine that could be used in a space station.

FAMOUS NAMES IN SPACE TRAVEL

In 1957, the first satellite, *Sputnik*, was launched, and in 1959 a USSR space probe took the first pictures of the dark side of the Moon. Then, in 1961, a Russian astronaut called Yuri Gagarin was the first human being into space. He orbited the Earth in a spacecraft and came back to Earth as a hero.

▲ There was a lot of competition between the USA and the USSR at that time to see who could land the first person on the Moon. The Americans won. In 1969, Neil Armstrong and Ed Aldrin landed on the Moon in their spacecraft *Apollo*. Neil Armstrong first set boot on the Moon and said his famous words: 'One small step for man, one giant leap for mankind.'

They brought back many pieces of Moon rock to study.

In 1991, Helen Sharman became the first British person to orbit the Earth. She travelled in the *Soyuz* capsule to the *Mir* space station, circling 350 km up. Her journey lasted for ten days – in that time she was able to help with many important experiments that can be done only where there is no weight.

What do you think space travellers in the future will achieve? Will they land on Mars?

▲ In 1984, an American astronaut called Bruce McCandliss became the first human satellite. He flew about 100 m from the Space Shuttle in a special hand-controlled unit that looks a bit like a flying armchair – what a way to travel!

WOW!
At one time, dogs led the race! A dog called Laika was the first living creature to travel in space. In 1957 Laika was launched in a rocket by the USSR. Sadly, she died when her oxygen supply ran out.

GLOSSARY

Asteroids   Lumps of material of different sizes that orbit the Sun, mostly between Mars and Jupiter.

Atmosphere   The blanket of gas around the Earth or other planets.

Axis   The imaginary line through the centre of a globe or sphere, for example the Earth's axis from North to South Pole.

Black hole   A place in the universe where gravity is so strong that nothing can escape from its pull, not even light.

Comet   A mixture of rock and ice that orbits the Sun. If a comet comes near the Sun, the heat makes a glowing tail.

Constellation   A pattern that people can see in the stars if they use their imagination, for example the Great Bear.

Corona   The halo of hot dust and gas around the Sun that can be seen during a total eclipse.

Eclipse   When the Moon casts a shadow on the Earth (eclipse of the Sun), or the Earth throws a shadow onto the Moon (eclipse of the Moon).

Ellipse   The curved shape, like a flat rugby ball, of a planet's orbit.

Exosphere   The outer layer of the atmosphere before 'space'.

Friction   The resistance when two things move across each other in different directions.

Galaxy   A collection of stars. Some galaxies have several million stars, others have thousands of million.

Gravity   The pulling force between two objects. You notice it only when one of the objects is massive, like the Earth or Sun.

Light-year   The distance travelled by a ray of light in one year (9.5 million million km).

Month   A lunar month (about twenty-eight days) is the time it takes for the Moon to go once round the Earth.

Nebula   A large cloud of dust or gas, or a mixture of both. A nebula is the birthplace of stars.

Orbit   The curved path that a satellite follows around the Earth or a planet follows around the Sun.

Pulsar   A distant star that gives off radio waves in short 'pulses'.

Quasar   A faint, star-like object far away from Earth.

Radiation   Energy that is sent out in waves.

Red Giant   An old star that is getting bigger and turning red.

Satellite   An object that goes round and round (orbits) another one, for example our Moon around the Earth.

Shooting star (meteor)   Not a star, but a streak of light seen when a meteoroid (a small lump of rock) burns up as it rushes into the Earth's atmosphere from space.

Star   A giant ball of gas, giving out light, heat and other rays.

Sunspot   A cool, dark patch on the Sun's surface.

Year   The time it takes for the Earth to go once round the Sun.

BOOKS TO READ

There are dozens of books about space and space travel. Here are just a few of the ones that my daughters and I like best:

The Big Book of Stars and Planets by Robin Kerrod (Octopus 1990)
Earth in Space by Robert Stephenson and Roger Browne (Wayland 1991)
Galaxies and Quasars by Heather Couper and Nigel Henbest (Franklin Watts 1986)
Galileo by Douglas McTavish (Wayland 1991)
The Inner Planets by Neil Ardley (Heinemann 1991)
Junior Illustrated Encyclopaedia: The Universe by James Muirden (Kingfisher 1987)
The Kingfisher Facts and Records Book of Space by Stuart Atkinson (Kingfisher 1990)
Our Future in Space by Tim Furniss (Wayland 1985)
Our Universe by Terry Jennings (OUP 1989)
The Outer Planets by Neil Ardley (Heinemann 1991)
Planet Earth and the Universe by Duncan Brewer (Cherrytree 1992)
Space Travel by Robin Kerrod (Wayland 1991)
The Stars by Heather Couper (Franklin Watts 1985)
The Usborne Book of Space Facts by Struan Reid (Usborne 1987)
The Young Astronomer by Ian Ridpath (Hamlyn 1985)

INDEX